DANNEA NELSON

From Page to Screen

The Best Mystery Novel Adaptations of All Time

Contents

1	Introduction	1
2	Historical Mysteries	5
3	Noir Mysteries	11
4	Locked-Room Mysteries	17
5	Detectives & Criminals	23
6	Thrillers	29
7	Conclusion	36
8	Resources	37

1

Introduction

The adaptation of a novel to a film or TV show is something we're all familiar with. We tend to have complex feelings over those adaptations because we are comparing our experience with the novel to our experience watching the same story unfold on the screen. This emotional reaction can be negative or positive depending on a number of factors: how closely or loosely the film follows the story from the page, how well the actors on the screen fit the characters as we've imagined them (if we've read the book first), how well the film conveys the novel's formal elements such as theme, style, and tone.

It is important to remember that reading a novel and watching a film are two distinct activities and lead us to the equivalent of "Which is better apple pie or New York strip?" The answer will depend on our own tastes, the quality of the product, and our needs at the time. So, as with these two different eating experiences, the ability to analyze a novel to film adaptation comes with limitations and personal tastes. Analyzing these adaptations becomes more than answering the assumed question of which is better.

A Concise History of Mystery Novels

While some argue that Edgar Allen Poe started the genre with "The Murders in the Rue Morgue" in 1841, there is evidence of Chinese crime fiction from nearly a millennium before him (Bailey 2). No matter its first appearance, one can argue that crime fiction now spans the globe; almost every country has a cadre of crime fiction writers, some better known than others.

Initially, mystery novels and short stories (also known as crime fiction) were deemed as entertainment for the lower social classes and lacked any artistic value (Plain 2008 4). However, within the last twenty years, scholars have recognized that the genre "offers a complex and very accurate portrayal of the society it is produced in, with each text becoming an exercise on reflection and morality" (Álvarez 140).

A Short History of Adaptations

Hollywood did not create the practice of adapting written materials to performance arts. Greek dramatists adapted myth stories that had been passed down through oral storytelling. Shakespeare appropriated various source material for his plays.

And when film came along, filmmakers recognized the value of a "good story" and began adapting plays, short stories, and novels for the screen.

There remains the difference though of the experience of reading a story on the page and that of sitting in a theater or on our couch watching an adaptation. As George Bluestone wrote:

> We observe that the word symbols in written language must be translated into images of things, feelings and concepts through the process of thought. Where the moving picture comes to us directly through perception, language must be fulfilled through the screen of conceptual apprehension (3).

In this book, we will focus on the best film adaptations of mystery stories broken into sub-genres: Historical, Noir, Locked Room, Detective, and Thriller. Within each of these sections, the films will be discussed in chronological order.

I hope you enjoy it!

2

Historical Mysteries

Historical mysteries are usually set in a time period that is considered historical from the reader's perspective with the central plot involving the solving of a mystery or crime.

The Moonstone

One of the earliest mystery stories to be recognized as a beacon of the genre is *The Moonstone* by Wilkie Collins. Written in 1868, it is widely considered to be the first full-length detective novel in the English language.

The story begins in India during the height of the expansion of the British Empire, and revolves around a large, yellow diamond which is the centerpiece of an idol to Chandra, the Hindu god of the Moon. Three Brahmins (priests) stand guard at all times. Colonel John Herncastle, while fighting for the British Army, kills the Brahmins and steals the gem even though he is warned that the diamond will exact its vengeance on him and anyone else who obtains it.

We shift forward in time to the mid-1800s. Herncastle was angry at his family, who shunned him, so he left the diamond in his will as a birthday gift to his niece Rachel. Rachel's eighteenth birthday is celebrated with a large party at which the guests include her cousin Franklin Blake. She wears the Moonstone that evening for all to see. Later that night the diamond is stolen from Rachel's bedroom, and a period of turmoil, unhappiness, misunderstandings and ill luck ensues. Told by a series of narratives from some of the main characters, the complex plot traces the subsequent efforts to explain the theft, identify the thief, trace the stone and recover it.

The Moonstone has been adapted a number of times beginning in 1934 when it was first made into a film by Monogram Pictures Corporation. However, the two best adaptations are the 1972 and 1996 BBC made for television serials, both titled as *The Moonstone*.

The Hound of the Baskervilles

In 1901, Arthur Conan Doyle's Sherlock Holmes returned to the page in *The Hound of the Baskervilles*. The story was first serialized in the magazine *The Strand* and, in 1902, was published as a novel.

James Mortimer introduces Holmes and his friend, Dr. John Watson, to an 18th century manuscript that recounts the myth of one, Hugo Baskerville. According to an old legend, the Baskerville family has been haunted by a curse since the time of the English Civil War, when Hugo Baskerville abducted and caused the death of a young woman on the moor, only to be killed in turn by a huge demonic hound. The same creature has, the story goes, been haunting the manor ever since, causing the premature death of many Baskerville heirs. Sir Charles believed in the plague of the hound and so does Mortimer, who now fears for the next in line, Sir Henry Baskerville.

Holmes dispatches his good friend Dr. Watson to accompany the young man to the family estate while he attends to other matters in London. Once there, Sir Henry meets the lovely Beryl Stapleton and her brother, John. The servants are acting strangely and, when Watson catches one of them signaling to someone on the moor, he thinks he knows who might be involved. Holmes, who has been masquerading as a tramp out on the moor, has his own ideas however. In the end, the solution to the mystery lies in the Baskerville family history.

The best adaptation of *The Hound of the Baskervilles* is the 1988 made for television movie starring Jeremy Brett as Sherlock Holmes and Edward Hardwicke as Dr. Watson. In a close second place, the 1939 movie version of *The Hound of the Baskervilles* with Basil Rathbone as Holmes and Nigel Bruce as Watson.

Rebecca

Daphne du Maurier published *Rebecca* in 1938 and the novel has never gone out of print. Du Maurier herself, adapted it to a stage play the following year.

The novel's narrator is an unnamed woman, naïve and in her early 20s, who impetuously marries a wealthy Englishman named Maxim de Winter, who is a 42-year-old widower. The narrator is soon convinced that Maxim regrets his impetuous decision to marry her and is still deeply in love with the seemingly perfect first Mrs. de Winter, Rebecca, who died in a sailing accident about a year before Maxim and the second Mrs. de Winter met. Both Maxim and the neighborhood near his beautiful estate Manderley are haunted by the memory of his late first wife.

In 1940, Alfred Hitchcock directed an Academy Award-winning film adaptation of *Rebecca* which starred Lawrence Olivier as Maxim de Winter and Joan Fontaine as the second Mrs. de Winter and is the best adaptation of the novel. If you prefer a more recent film, Lily James and Armie Hammer star in the 2020 Netflix production of *Rebecca*.

Laura

Another classic, single name mystery is *Laura*, published in 1943 by Vera Caspary. It ran in *Colliers* from October to November

1942 as a seven-part serial titled *Ring Twice for Laura* and was published in book form the next year.

Laura is narrated in the first person by several alternating characters. These individual stories all revolve around the apparent murder of the title character, a successful New York advertiser, killed in the doorway of her apartment with a shotgun blast that obliterated her face.

When Detective Mark McPherson is assigned the case, he focuses on the two men who were prominent in Laura's life: her former lover, Waldo Lydecker, a narcissistic middle-aged writer and her fiance, the philandering Shelby Carpenter. But who would have wanted to kill a girl with whom every man she met seemed to fall in love? To make matters worse, McPherson finds himself falling under her spell too. Then one night, halfway through his investigations, something seriously bizarre happens to make him rethink the whole case.

Caspary sold the film rights for *Laura* to Twentieth Century Fox, leading to Gene Tierney portraying the 1944 movie adaptation. She was joined by Dana Andrews as McPherson, Clifton Webb as Lydecker, and Vincent Price as Carpenter.

3

Noir Mysteries

Noir generally refers to crime style novels and films of the 1940s and 50s. These movies are sometimes referred to as "hardboiled" detective stories. More recent versions are labeled as Neo-Noir.

The Maltese Falcon

Initially serialized in *Black Mask* magazine, beginning with the September 1929 issue, *The Maltese Falcon* by Dashiell Hammet was published as a novel in 1930.

Hammet's novel opens in the office of Spade and Archer, the San Francisco detective agency of Sam Spade and Miles Archer. The two men are partners, but Sam doesn't like Miles much. A beautiful woman, who goes by the name of Miss Wonderly, walks into their office and by that night, everything's changed.

Miles is dead, as is a man named Floyd Thursby. It seems Miss Wonderly is surrounded by dangerous men: Joel Cairo, who uses gardenia-scented calling cards and Kasper Gutman, with his enormous girth and feigned civility. Her only hope of protection comes from Spade, who becomes a suspect in at least one murder. More murders follow, all because of the small statue of a bird - the Maltese Falcon.

While the novel has been adapted into movies three times, the best is the third one, released in 1941. The film was directed by John Huston and starred Humphrey Bogart as Sam Spade.

The Big Sleep

This novel introduces author Raymond Chandler's famous private investigator, Philip Marlowe. *The Big Sleep*, published in 1939, is noted for its complexity, with characters double-crossing one another and secrets being exposed throughout the narrative.

Wealthy and ailing General Sternwood hires Private Detective Philip Marlowe to handle a blackmail perpetrated against the General's younger of two daughters, wild Carmen, for collection of purported gambling debts. This blackmail is the second such situation in which Carmen has found herself in recent history. The first was resolved when the General paid. That time, it was handled by the General's companion Sean Regan, who had left a month previously without a word. Rumors indicate that Regan has run off with the blond wife of casino owner Eddie Mars. During his investigation, Marlowe discovers that he's entangled in a complex web of lies and deceit.

The best adaptation of *The Big Sleep* is the 1946 version starring Humphrey Bogart as Marlowe and Lauren Bacall as Vivian. Interestingly, the renowned author, William Faulkner, one of the 20th century's most gifted novelists, is credited as one of the screenplay writers.

Strangers on a Train

Published in 1950, *Strangers on a Train* was Patricia Highsmith's highly regarded debut novel. She went on to write several other novels which have also been adapted to the screen.

Two strangers, Guy Haines, an architect, and Charles Anthony Bruno, a psychopathic playboy, meet by chance on a train. After they each complain about the presence in his life of someone he'd rather be rid of, Bruno suggests they exchange murders. Bruno will kill Haines's wife so he can marry the woman he loves, then Haines can kill Bruno's father. There would be no chance of getting caught because there would be no motive found.

While Guy doesn't take him seriously, Bruno follows through with killing Haines' wife while he is in Mexico. Haines struggles with guilt and implicating himself and is eventually pressured by Bruno to kill the latter's father. The stress, guilt, and deceit continue to spiral leading to a confrontation between the two strangers.

Alfred Hitchcock's psychological noir thriller, the best of many adaptations of *Strangers on a Train*, was released in movie theaters in 1951. The American Film Institute's '100 Years… 100 Thrills' listing of the top 100 most exciting movies in American cinema includes *Strangers on a Train* at #32.

L.A. Confidential

In 1990, *L.A. Confidential*, the third installment of James Ellroy's L.A. Quartet series was published to rave reviews.

The story features three protagonists who are members of the Los Angeles police department in the early 1950s: Edmund Exley whose father was a cop and is a "straight arrow" who informs on other officers in a police brutality scandal; Wendell "Bud" White, an intimidating enforcer with a fixation on men who abuse women; and Jack Vincennes, who acts as more of a celebrity than a cop who is also a technical advisor on a police television show and provides tips to a scandal magazine.

Exley, White, and Vincennes must bury their differences to work through the events of a massacre at a coffee shop with connections to organized crime, political corruption, heroin trafficking, pornography, prostitution and Hollywood.

The 1997 film adaptation was an acclaimed success and nominated for nine Academy Awards. It starred Kevin Spacey, Russell Crowe, Guy Pearce, James Cromwell, Kim Basinger, David Strathairn and Danny DeVito.

Shutter Island

Shutter Island is a novel by Dennis Lehane that was first published in April 2003. Lehane has said he sought to write a novel that would be an homage to Gothic settings, B movies, and pulp (Weich).

Over the course of several days in 1954, Federal Marshal Edward "Teddy" Daniels and his new partner Chuck Aule travel to a government-run institution for the criminally insane on Shutter Island, near Boston, to investigate a report that a prisoner has gone missing. Traumatized from what he saw during his time as a soldier during World War II, Daniels is also haunted by his wife's more recent death in a fire.

The investigation provides a promising lead, but the institution refuses the partners access to records they suspect would break the case wide open. As a hurricane cuts off communication with the mainland, more dangerous criminals "escape" in the confusion, and the puzzling, improbable clues multiply. During the chaos and troubled by severe migraines, Daniels begins to doubt everything - his memory, his partner, even his own sanity.

Martin Scorsese directed the 2010 film adaptation of *Shutter Island* that starred Leonardo DiCaprio as Teddy Daniels and Mark Ruffalo as Chuck Aule. The film opened at #1 at the US box office.

4

Locked-Room Mysteries

Also known as "impossible crime" mysteries, "locked-room" mysteries typically involve a murder committed in circumstances under which it is seemingly impossible for the perpetrator not only to commit the crime but to evade detection in getting in to and out of the crime scene.

Murder on the Orient Express

Agatha Christie first introduced the Belgian detective Hercule Poirot in her first detective novel, *The Mysterious Affair at Styles*, which was published in 1920. *Murder on the Orient Express*, featuring Poirot's continued exploits, is a work of detective fiction by Agatha Christie. It was first published in 1934.

In *Murder on the Orient Express*, Poirot finds himself unexpectedly returning to London on the famous train along with a large cast of interesting and deceitful passengers. Early the following morning, the passengers are informed that the train is stuck in a snowdrift and there are workers on their way to get the train out.

Overnight, a passenger is murdered, and the murderer is still aboard, having no way to escape in the snow. Using his remarkable powers of observation and his "little grey cells," Poirot embarks on discovering who the murderer is.

There are a few adaptations of *Murder on the Orient Express*; however, the TV series *Agatha Christie's Poirot: The Early Cases Collection*, which ran from 1989 to 2013, featured *Murder on the Orient* in a 2010 episode. The show features the finest portrayal of Poirot by David Suchet. Another excellent adaptation is the 1974 movie, *Murder on the Orient Express*, starring Albert Finney, Lauren Bacall, Ingrid Bergman, and Sean Connery.

Death on the Nile

Another Christie novel that featured Poirot, *Death on the Nile*, is set on a luxury boat navigating the Nile River in Egypt for a wedding party. It was initially published in 1937.

While on holiday in Egypt, Poirot is invited to join the wedding celebration of an heiress, Linette Doyle née Ridgeway, and her new husband, Simon Doyle. Linette asks Poirot to persuade her former friend Jacqueline de Bellefort to stop stalking her and Simon, who also happens to be Jacqueline's former fiancé.

There is an altercation between Jacqueline and Simon, in which she shoots him in the leg. The following morning, Linette is found dead in her cabin. This tale of unbridled passion and jealousy features a group of well-off travelers and wicked turns as Poirot works to determine who murdered Linette and why.

The best adaptation of this Agatha Christie classic is the 1978 film starring Peter Ustinov as the famed detective Poirot. Another excellent adaptation is the more recent film directed by and starring Kenneth Branagh as Poirot, Gal Gadot as Linette, Armie Hammer as Simon, and Emma Mackey as Jacqueline.

And Then There Were None

In 1939, Agatha Christie's *And Then There Were None* (originally titled after a children's counting song with a problematic title in today's world) was published in the United Kingdom. The title used here is the one used for the first United States edition, published in 1940.

The story begins with the arrival of 8 guests to a small, isolated island, each having received an unexpected personal invitation. They are met by the butler and cook-housekeeper, Thomas and Ethel Rogers, who explain that their hosts have not yet arrived, though they have left instructions.

One by one, the 10 individuals are killed in a manner which reflects one of the lines of the children's rhyme. Scotland Yard officials arrive to begin investigating and reconstructing the deaths with the help of the victims' diaries and a coroner's report.

The British adaptation that aired as *And Then There Were None* on BBC One in 2015 and was produced in cooperation with Acorn Media and Agatha Christie Productions, is the best. It was also the first English language adaptation featuring an ending similar to that of the novel.

Evil Under the Sun

This 1941 Agatha Christie novel features Hercules Poirot who has taken a holiday at a secluded hotel in Devon, England.

Poirot finds himself surrounded by hotel guests who turn out to be an intriguing lot, with infidelity and hatred abounding. The center of much of the deception and upheaval is Arlena Marshall, the wife of wealthy Lionel Marshall and step-mother to his daughter, Linda. Poirot notes that Arlena is extremely flirtatious and causes anger in nearly everyone, including her step-daughter.

When Arlena is found murdered at Pixy Cove near the hotel, everyone is a suspect, even with their seemingly airtight alibis.

Topping the list of best adaptations is, once again, the TV series *Agatha Christie's Poirot: The Early Cases Collection*, which aired the *Evil Under the Sun* episode in 2003. Although the 1982 movie adaptation starring Peter Ustinov is also very highly regarded.

Crooked House

Agatha Christie's *Crooked House*, published in 1949, the title being a reference to the children's rhyme "There Was a Crooked Man." It is one of just a handful of Christie novels that were published in the United States before being published in the United Kingdom.

This novel introduces us to three generations of the Leonides family who live together under the roof of "Three Gables," the manor home of Aristide, the wealthy patriarch and his second wife, Brenda. She is decades his junior and suspected of having an affair with Laurence, the grandchildren's tutor. Aristide's first wife Marcia died and her sister Edith has cared for the household since then.

After Aristide is poisoned, his granddaughter Sophia tells narrator and fiancé Charles Hayward that they cannot marry until the killer is found out. Charles's father, "The Old Man", is Assistant Commissioner of Scotland Yard, so Charles is allowed to investigate along with assigned detective Chief Inspector Taverner.

The movie adaptation of *Crooked House* was released in 2017 and stars Stefanie Martini, Max Irons, Terrence Stamp, Glen Close, Gillian Anderson, Christina Hendricks, and Julian Sands.

5

Detectives & Criminals

T hese stories feature detectives, both professional and amatuer, working to unravel crimes and murders, even when those detective figures are also criminals.

To Catch a Thief

David Dodge became a writer when he bet his wife that he could write a better mystery novel than the ones they were reading during a rainy vacation. *To Catch a Thief* was his first stand-alone book and the most successful of his career primarily because Alfred Hitchcock bought the film rights before it was published early in 1952.

To Catch a Thief is set in 1951 and features retired jewel thief John Robie also known as "Le Chat" or "The Cat" due to his daring and athletic heists along the French Riviera's hotels and villas. Robie has been living quietly in his villa, tending its garden, and spending time with his neighbors when a Le Chat-styled burglar begins stealing those neighbors' jewelry.

In order to clear his name and avoid being arrested for crimes he did not commit, Robie joins forces with his police friend, former criminal friends, and the daughter of one of the theft victims, Frances Stevens.

Alfred Hitchcock's Academy Award nominated 1955 film, *To Catch a Thief*, starred Cary Grant as John Robie and Grace Kelly as Frances.

D'entre les Mortes (The Living and the Dead)

The French crime fiction writing duo of Pierre Boileau and Pierre Ayraud aka Thomas Narcejac wrote a novel entitled *D'entre les Mortes* that was published in France in 1954. It was first published in English in 1956 as *The Living and the Dead* from a translation by Geoffrey Sainsbury.

In 1940, during the World War II German assault on Paris, lawyer Roger Flavières is asked by his longtime friend Gevigne to watch over his wife (who seems to be suffering from some mental health problem) because he is extremely busy at the moment with his business concerns. Flavières agrees and strikes up a friendship with Gevigne's wife, Madeleine.

Unfortunately, she is determined to go to a village outside of

Paris to climb a church belltower. Flavières is unable to follow due to an extreme fear of heights and he watches helplessly as Madeleine falls to her death. A few years later, Flavières sees a woman who looks remarkably like Madeleine and determines that he needs the whole story from her.

Another brilliant film from Alfred Hitchcock, it was released in 1958 as *Vertigo*. Hitchcock changed things a bit, as the movie was loosely based on the French novel rather than a true adaptation. It starred James "Jimmy" Stewart, Kim Novak, and Barbara Bel Geddes.

The Godfather

In 1969, Mario Puzo published his best known novel, *The Godfather*, which he also co-adapted into the film trilogy directed by Francis Ford Coppola.

The novel details the life of Vito Corleone who is the head, *The Godfather*, of one of five Mafia families in New York City. After World War II, the families were at war for control of the city. When Vito is shot, his sons, Santino and Michael take over, but Santino is killed leaving control solely in Michael's hands.

Michael plans his revenge and relocates the family's power base to Las Vegas. The move to Nevada furthers his goal to legitimize the family and get them out of organized crime. He sells all of the family's remaining businesses in New York and permanently relocates the family to Las Vegas.

The Godfather is widely considered to be one of the best films ever made. The film and its leading actor, Marlon Brando, won Academy and Golden Globe Awards. It was also hugely successful at the box office.

Six Days of the Condor

The 1974 novel, *Six Days of the Condor*, by James Grady is a suspense drama set in then-contemporary Washington, D.C. and was his debut.

Six Days of the Condor features Ronald Malcolm as its hero. He spends his days as a CIA clandestine operations office worker, analyzing the plots of mystery and spy novels. When he returns from slipping out to lunch one day, he finds his entire section murdered. Malcolm phones in the emergency and gives his codename "Condor" to the person on the other end of the line.

When he attempts to "come in" for protection, the agent he meets attempts to kill him, so he goes on the run. He enlists the help of a paralegal named Wendy Ross and the two of them attempt to get to the bottom of the conspiracy.

The 1975 adaptation called *Three Days of the Condor* was loosely based on the novel and starred Robert Redford, Faye Dunaway, Cliff Robertson, and Max von Sydow. While much was changed from the novel, this is an excellent movie.

Gone Baby Gone

Gone Baby Gone, published in 1998, is the fourth in a series by Dennis Lehane set in Boston, Massachusetts.

Private investigators and couple Patrick Kenzie and Angie Gennaro are approached by a woman who wants them to find her missing niece, Amanda McCready. During their search, they come to discover that the girl's mother, Helene, had taken Amanda along while she and her then boyfriend Skinny Ray stole two hundred thousand dollars from an imprisoned drug dealer.

Patrick and Angie discover that the whole kidnapping had been orchestrated as part of a scheme involving a small ring of police who take children from abusive and neglectful homes to then place them with caring and attentive parents. This discovery ultimately turns into a crisis for Patrick and Angie, both professionally and personally.

Casey Affleck and Michelle Monaghan starred in the 2007 movie adaptation of *Gone Baby Gone*. Not only was the film Ben Affleck's directorial debut, but he was also one of the writers.

6

Thrillers

Thrillers are referred to as edge-of-your-seat stories because they elicit heightened feelings of suspense, excitement, surprise, anticipation and anxiety in readers. Their plots are often driven by a villain and obstacles that the protagonist must overcome. There is almost always some sort of cover-up of important information as well.

The Silence of the Lambs

In 1988, Thomas Harris's *The Silence of the Lambs* hit book-shelves. It was the sequel to his 1981 novel, *Red Dragon*, both featuring the cannibalistic serial killer Dr. Hannibal Lecter.

A young FBI trainee named Clarice Starling is asked to present a questionnaire to the brilliant, yet criminally insane forensic psychiatrist Dr. Hannibal Lector who is serving nine consecutive life sentences for a series of cannibalistic murders. Jack Crawford, who heads the FBI's Behavioral Analysis Unit, sends Starling because he believes she can convince Lector to help with a case involving another serial killer dubbed "Buffalo Bill."

Throughout the investigation, Starling periodically returns to Lecter in search of information, and the two form a give-and-take relationship in which he offers her cryptic clues about "Buffalo Bill" in return for information about her childhood as an orphan.

The Silence of the Lambs was adapted for the screen in 1991 by Jonathan Demme and won Academy Awards for Best Picture, Best Director, Best Screenplay, Best Actor and Best Actress. It starred Jodie Foster as Clarice Starling and Anthony Hopkins as Hannibal Lecter.

The Da Vinci Code

Dan Brown's second novel featuring professor of symbology Robert Langdon, *The Da Vinci Code*, was published in 2003 and was almost immediately deemed controversial due to its story presenting an alternative religious history. One whose central plot point speculated that the Holy Grail legend and Mary Magdalene's role in the history of Christianity were not what organized religions would have us believe.

The Da Vinci Code begins with the murder of the curator of the Louvre museum in Paris, Jacques Saunière. When his body is found, posed in the manner of Da Vinci's *Vitruvian Man*, the police ask Harvard professor Robert Langdon, who happens to be in Paris on business, to decode the cryptic message the curator left during the final moments of his life.

Langdon and Sophie Neveu, who is Saunière's estranged granddaughter and a police cryptologist, work together to follow the clues to unravel Saunière's message and the mystery behind Da Vinci's code.

Academy Award winning director Ron Howard's film *The Da Vinci Code* hit screens in 2006, starring Tom Hanks as Robert Langdon and Audrey Tautou as Sophie Neveu.

The Girl with the Dragon Tattoo

The Swedish author, Stieg Larsson, titled the book *Män som hatar kvinnor*, which literally translates to *Men Who Hate Women*. He refused to allow his Swedish publisher to change the title before publishing the novel. However, after his untimely death in 2004, the English publisher changed the title to *The Girl with the Dragon Tattoo* prior to its publication in 2008.

The novel begins with the middle-aged Mikael Blomkvist who publishes a magazine in Stockholm, losing a libel case against him and facing three months in prison. Facing jail time and professional disgrace, Blomkvist steps down from his position on the magazine's board of directors. Blomkvist receives a freelance assignment from Henrik Vanger, the elderly former CEO of Vanger Enterprises, to use his journalist skills to solve the cold case of his great niece who disappeared 40 years earlier.

Teaming up with gifted private investigator Lisbeth Salander, the titular character, Blomkvist begins analyzing 40 years worth of information surrounding the Vanger family. The duo, under the pretext of researching the family history, soon becomes acquainted with the members of the extended Vanger family who are variously mad, uninterested, concerned, hostile, or aloof.

The Swedish-language and the English-language film adaptations, released in 2009 and 2011 respectively, have received the same 7.8/10 IMDb User scores on the Internet Movie Database website.

Gone Girl

Gillian Flynn wrote the 2012 novel *Gone Girl* and its 2014 film adaptation. The adaptation earned her nominations for the Golden Globe, Writers Guild of America Award, and BAFTA Award for Best Adapted Screenplay.

The novel is centered on former New York-based writer Nick Dunne who has become a small town Missouri creative writing professor and his wife, Amy. The narrative switches between Nick's point of view and Amy's. Nick's narration begins shortly after arriving home on their fifth wedding anniversary to find Amy missing from their home and signs of a struggle. Amy's narration comes in the form of her diaries and follows the earlier stages of their relationship.

Following the move to Missouri to help care for Nick's mother, their marriage begins to deteriorate. Amy hates being a housewife in the suburbs and resents Nick for making her move. Her diary portrays Nick as an aggressive, moody, idle, and threatening husband, and indicates that she fears for her life. Nick and Amy are unreliable narrators who each have secrets that are revealed as the story unfolds.

In 2014, the film adaptation of *Gone Girl*, also written by Gillian Flynn, was released to critical and financial success. The film starred Ben Affleck as Nick Dunne and Rosamund Pike as his wife Amy Dunne née Elliott. Pike's performance garnered nominations for an Academy Award, BAFTA Award, Golden Globe Award, and Screen Actors Guild Award for Best Actress.

The Girl on the Train

The Girl on the Train, written by Paula Hawkins, was published in 2015. The film rights were acquired before the book was published and it debuted at #1 on *The New York Times* Fiction Best Sellers list.

The narration of *The Girl on the Train* is told from the viewpoints of three women: Rachel Watson, Anna Watson, and Megan Hipwell, all of whom are unreliable narrators. Rachel is an alcoholic who frequently binges to the point of blacking out and harasses her ex-husband, Tom, and his new wife, oftentimes having no recollection of doing so. Anna is the new wife who resents Rachel's harassment. Megan is the wife of a couple that Rachel sees from the train window on a daily basis. Rachel idealizes their life and calls them "Jason" and "Jess" in her head.

One day, Rachel is stunned to see "Jess," whose name is actually Megan, kissing another man. The next day, after another binge and blackout, Rachel awakens to find herself bloody and hurt with no memories of how she got that way. She learns that Megan is missing, and is questioned by the police after Anna reports having seen her drunkenly staggering around the neighborhood the night of Megan's disappearance. Rachel is determined to discover what is hidden in her memory to help solve what happened to Megan.

The film adaptation was released in 2016 and is pretty faithful to the novel. It starred Emily Blunt as Rachel Watson, Rebecca Ferguson as Anna Watson, and Haley Bennett as Megan Hipwell.

7

Conclusion

There it is, a list of some of the best page-to-screen mystery novel adaptations of all time. Whether you're into tense thrillers or historical mysteries, there's something for everyone. This list is compiled from a number of sources found below and is in no way definitive or all-encompassing. As I stated in the Introduction, "best" is subjective and formed through our own tastes and needs at the time, in addition to the perceived quality of the product itself. You may agree or disagree with my choices and that's okay because it's to be expected. Hopefully, though, you've learned something or were exposed to a different point of view that expanded your mind.

Please, if you enjoyed this book and found it helpful, I would be very appreciative if you would leave a favorable review on Amazon. Thanks!

8

Resources

Alvarez. (2019). Criminal Readings: The Transformative and Instructive Power of Crime Fiction. *Journal of Comparative Literature and Aesthetics*, *42*(4), 142–152.

Bailey, F. Y. (2017). Crime Fiction. *Oxford Research Encyclopedia of Criminology and Criminal Justice*. http://doi.org/10.1093/acrefore/9780190264079.013.29

Bluestone, G. (1957). *Novels into Film*. University of California Press.

Brandman, M. (2021, November 1). *The 10 Greatest Movies Adapted from Crime Novels—According to a Producer and Novelist*. CrimeReads. Retrieved July 20, 2022, from http://crimereads.com/the-10-greatest-movies-adapted-from-crime-novels-according-to-a-producer-and-novelist/

Hicks, K. (2022, March 15). *Best Murder Mystery Movies Based on Books, Ranked*. MovieWeb. Retrieved July 21, 2022, from http://movieweb.com/murder-mystery-movies-based-on-books/

IMDb, an Amazon Company. (n.d.). *IMDb: Ratings, Reviews, and Where to Watch the Best Movies & TV Shows*. IMDb. Retrieved July 20, 2022, from https://www.imdb.com/

Ranker.com. (2022, July 20). *The Most Intriguing Mystery Movies Based on Novels*. Ranker. Retrieved July 20, 2022, from http://www.ranker.com/list/best-mystery-movies-based-on-books/ranker-film

The Home of Agatha Christie. (2018, August 2). *Quotes from Hercule Poirot*. Agatha Christie. Retrieved July 21, 2022, from http://www.agathachristie.com/news/2018/eight-quotes-from-hercule-poirot

Tony-Scheinman. (2019, November 27). *BEST MYSTERY FILMS BASED ON A NOVEL*. IMDb. Retrieved July 20, 2022, from http://www.imdb.com/list/ls025880637/

Weich, D. (2007, December 22). *Dennis Lehane Meets the Bronte Sisters*. Powell's Books Online. Retrieved July 20, 2022, from archived at http://www.powells.com/authors/lehane.html